Simone Weil
Wrestling with God

In trying to understand her, we must not be distracted – as is only too likely to happen on first reading – by considering how far, and at what points, we agree or disagree. We must simply expose ourselves to the personality of a woman of genius, of a kind of genius akin to that of the saints.

    T. S. Eliot, Preface, *The Need for Roots*, p. vi

Portrait of Simone Weil
by David Lowe

Simone Weil

Wrestling with God

Selected and Translated by
Gerald A. Buss

HartWorks
2017

For Joe

Transfiguration

I think he needs none
I think he has had one
He remains in a state
A condition of kindness
Lives in light bright as the sun

2014 August 6
Feast of the Transfiguration

Contents

Simone : Page 6

Attente de Dieu
In Expectation of God
Page 7

Écrits de Londres
London Writings
Page 85

Lettre à un religieux
Letter to a Priest
Page 103

La Pesanteur et la Grâce
Gravity & Grace
Page 157

Intuitions pré-Chrétiennes
Pre-Christian Intuitions
Page 263

———

Bibliography : Page 281

Other Works by the Translator : Page 295

Simone

Simone brings to mind
her song and her singing
of the right and the true
of identities of love
for God and for man
her search in texts
of East and West

Someone called her act
one of ransacking –
making her seem
a Visigoth or even a Hun
laying waste treasures
the while laying them out
in the light of the sun

2014 February 17

Attente de Dieu
In Expectation of God

Lettres[1]

Dieu récompense l'âme qui pense à lui avec attention et amour, et il la récompense en exerçant sur elle une contrainte rigoureusement, mathématiquement proportionelle à cette attention et amour. [15]

---

[1] *Attente de Dieu*, pp. 12-84.

Letters

God compensates the soul who thinks of him with attention and longing. He compensates that soul by setting in motion a divine attraction that is precisely, mathematically proportionate to the soul's attention and longing.

Je crois que seuls ceux qui sont au-dessus d'un certain niveau de spiritualité peuvent avoir part aux sacrements en tant que tels. Ceux qui sont au-dessous de ce niveau, quoi qu'ils fassent, aussi longtemps qu'ils ne l'ont pas atteint, n'appartiennent pas à proprement parler à l'Eglise. En ce qui me concerne, je pense être au-dessous de ce niveau. [17]

I believe that only those who are above a certain spiritual level can participate in the sacraments as such. Those who are below this level, whatever they might do and as long as they have not reached it, do not strictly speaking belong to the church. As for me I think that I am below this level.

[L]orsque je me représente concrètement et comme une chose qui pourrait être prochaine l'acte par lequel j'entrerais dans l'église, aucune pensée ne me fait plus de peine que celle de me séparer de la masse immense et malheureuse des incroyants. J'ai le besoin essentiel, et je crois pouvoir dire la vocation, de passer parmi les hommes et les différents milieux humains en me confondant avec eux, en prenant la même couleur, dans toute la mesure du moins où la conscience ne s'y oppose pas, en disparaissant parmi eux, cela afin qu'ils se montrent tels qu'ils sont et sans se déguiser pour moi. C'est que je désire les connaître afin de les aimer tels qu'ils sont. Car si je ne les aime pas tels qu'ils sont, ce n'est pas eux que j'aime, et mon amour n'est pas vrai. [19]

When I concretely represent to myself — as something that could take place in the near future — the act by which I would enter the church, nothing gives me more pain than the thought of separating myself from the huge unhappy mass of unbelievers. I have this essential need — I believe I could call it my vocation — to walk among diverse peoples, to share in a variety of human situations; to lose myself among them, to take on their coloration — at least to the extent that this would not be opposed to conscience; to disappear among them in order that they might show themselves as they are without their having to put on a mask for my sake. It's just that I desire to know them in order to love them as they are. For if I don't love them as they are, it's not them that I love, and my love is not real.

Ce n'est pas mon affaire de penser à moi. Mon affaire est de penser à Dieu. C'est à Dieu à penser à moi. [22]

It's not my business to think of myself. My business is to think of God. It's up to God to think of me.

Je crois qu'il ne sert à rien de combattre directement les faiblesses naturelles. Il faut se faire violence pour agir comme si on ne les avait pas dans les circonstances où un devoir l'exige impérieusement; et dans le cours ordinaire de la vie il faut bien les connaître, en tenir compte avec prudence, et s'efforcer d'en faire bon usage, car elles sont toutes susceptibles d'un bon usage. [24]

I do not believe that it serves any purpose to struggle directly against natural weaknesses. In those circumstances where a duty urgently demands it we must force ourselves to fulfill that duty as though these weaknesses did not exist. In the ordinary course of life we must be well aware of them, prudently taking them into account and forcing ourselves to make good use of them. It is possible for all of them to be put to some good use.

Des saints ont approuvé les Croisades, l'Inquisition. Je ne peux pas ne pas penser qu'ils ont eu tort. Je ne peux pas récuser la lumière de la conscience. Si je pense que sur un point je vois plus clair qu'eux, moi qui suis tellement loin au-dessous d'eux, je dois admettre que sur ce point ils ont été aveuglés par quelque chose de très puissant. Ce quelque chose, c'est l'église en tant que chose sociale. Si cette chose sociale leur a fait du mal, quel mal ne ferait-elle pas à moi, qui suis particulièrement vulnérable aux influences sociales, et qui suis presque infiniment plus faible qu'eux? [...] Il en résulte que le social est irréductiblement le domaine du diable [...] Par social je n'entends pas tout ce qui se rapporte à une cité, mais seulement les sentiments collectifs. [25]

There have been saints who gave their approval to the Crusades,[2] the Inquisition.[3] I cannot help but think that they were wrong. I cannot challenge the light of conscience. Even though I am far beneath them I think on this point I see more clearly than they did. On this point I have to conclude that they were blinded by something very powerful. This something is the church in its character as a social institution, a collective. If this social thing did them harm, what harm would it not do to me, I who am particularly vulnerable to social influences, I who am almost infinitely weaker than they were? [...] It follows from this that the social is irreducibly the domain of the devil [...] By social I do not mean everything that pertains to a society. I mean only the sentiments aroused within a collective setting.

---

[2] The Crusades were undertaken to liberate Jerusalem and other places sacred to Christian history; there were eight crusades, beginning in 1095 and ending in 1270.
[3] The Inquisition was an institution charged with eliminating heresy.

Je sens qu'il m'est nécessaire, qu'il m'est prescrit de me trouver seule, étrangère et en exil par rapport à n'importe quel milieu humain sans exception. [26]

I feel that it is necessary for me, that it is prescribed for me, to find myself alone, an outsider, an exile. This is true with respect to every human milieu without exception.

[I]l est impossible de penser à vous sans penser à Dieu. [32]

It is impossible to think of you without thinking of God.

[J]'ai toujours cru que l'instant de la mort est la norme et le but de la vie. Je pensais que pour ceux qui vivent comme il convient, c'est l'instant où pour une fraction infinitésimale du temps la vérité pure, nue, certaine, éternelle entre dans l'âme. [37]

I have always believed that the moment of death is the measurement and the goal of life. For those who live as they should I thought that it is the moment when — for the tiniest fraction of time — pure, naked, certain, eternal truth penetrates the soul.

Après des mois de ténèbres intérieures j'ai eu soudain et pour toujours la certitude que n'importe quel être humain, même si ses facultés naturelles sont presque nulles, pénètre dans ce royaume de la vérité réservée au génie, si seulement il désire la vérité et fait perpétuellement un effort d'attention pour l'atteindre [...] Sous le nom de vérité j'englobais aussi la beauté, la vertu et toute espèce de bien, de sorte qu'il s'agissait pour moi d'une conception du rapport entre la grâce et le désir. La certitude que j'avais reçue, c'était que quand on désire du pain on ne reçoit pas des pierres. [39]

After months of inner darkness I suddenly experienced a certitude that has become permanent: that every human being — no matter who, even if his natural abilities are almost non-existent — can penetrate this realm of truth reserved for genius, if only he desires truth and ceaselessly concentrates all his attention in order to attain it [...] In the word *truth* I also included beauty, virtue, and every kind of good, in such a way that for me it was a matter of seeing the relationship between grace and desire. The certitude that I had received was this: when we desire bread we do not receive stones.

[U]n jeune Anglais catholique [...] m'a fait connaître l'existence de ces poètes anglais du xviie siècle qu'on nomme métaphysiques. Plus tard, en les lisant, j'y ai découvert le poème [...] qui est intitulé *Amour*. Je l'ai appris par cœur. Souvent, au moment culminant des crises violentes de maux de tête, je me suis exercée à le réciter en y appliquant toute mon attention et en adhérant de toute mon âme à la tendresse qu'il enferme. Je croyais le réciter seulement comme un beau poème, mais à mon insu cette récitation avait la vertu d'une prière. C'est au cours d'une de ces récitations que, comme je vous l'ai écrit, le Christ lui-même est descendu et m'a prise. [43-45]

A young English Catholic [...] acquainted me with the existence of those 17th century English writers known as the "metaphysical poets."[4] Later, while reading them I discovered the poem [...] that is entitled *Love*.[5] I learned it by heart. Often at the most critical stage of one of my violent headaches I recited it with a completely concentrated attention, attaching all my soul to the tenderness it expresses. I believed that I was only reciting a beautiful poem but without my knowing it this recitation had the power of a prayer. It was in the course of one of these recitations that, as I've written you, Christ himself came down and took hold of me.

---

[4] A term used to designate certain English poets of the 17th century, including George Herbert, John Donne, Andrew Marvell, Henry Vaughn, and a few others.
[5] See this poem by George Herbert below on page 84.

[J]e ne lis autant que possible que ce dont j'ai faim, au moment où j'en ai faim, et alors je ne lis pas, je mange. [45]

As much as possible I read only what I have a hunger for, when I am hungry for it; and then I don't read, I eat.

[I]l me paraissait certain, et je le crois encore aujourd'hui, qu'on ne peut jamais trop résister à Dieu si on le fait par pur souci de la vérité. Le Christ aime qu'on lui préfère la vérité, car avant d'être le Christ il est la vérité. Si on détourne de lui pour aller vers la vérité, on ne fera pas un long chemin sans tomber dans ses bras. [45-46]

It seemed certain to me — and I still believe it today — that we can never wrestle too much with God so long as it is done out of pure concern for the truth. Christ desires us to prefer the truth to him because before being the Christ he is the truth. If we turn our backs on him to go in search of the truth we will not go far before falling into his arms.

Je récitais le *Pater* en grec chaque jour avant le travail, et je l'ai répété bien souvent dans la vigne. Depuis lors je me suis imposé pour unique practique de le réciter une fois chaque matin avec une attention absolue. Si pendant la récitation mon attention s'égare ou s'endort, fût-ce d'une manière infinitésimale, je recommence jusqu'à ce que j'aie obtenu une fois une attention absolument pure. Il m'arrive alors parfois de recommencer une fois encore par pur plaisir [...] La vertu de cette practique est extraordinaire et me surprend chaque fois, car quoique je l'éprouve chaque jour elle dépasse chaque fois mon attente. [48]

Every day before work I said the Lord's Prayer in Greek. While in the vineyard I repeated it quite often. Since that time I have imposed this singular exercise upon myself — saying it once every morning with a totally concentrated attention. If while saying it my mind wanders or dozes — even for a fraction of a moment — I begin again from the beginning until I have said it once with absolutely pure attention. Sometimes I say it once more for the pure pleasure of it [...] The power of this exercise is extraordinary and surprises me every time for, although I experience it daily, it always surpasses my expectation.

Parfois les premiers mots [du *Pater*] déjà arrachent ma pensée à mon corps et la transportent en un lieu hors de l'espace d'où il n'y a ni perspective ni point de vue. L'espace s'ouvre. L'infinité de l'espace ordinaire de la perception est remplacée par une infinité à la deuxième ou quelquefois troisième puissance. En même temps cette infinité d'infinité s'emplit de part en part de silence, un silence qui n'est pas une absence de son, qui est l'objet d'une sensation positive, plus positive que celle d'un son. Les bruits, s'il y en a, ne me parviennent qu'après avoir traversé ce silence. Parfois aussi, pendant cette récitation ou à d'autres moments, le Christ est présent en personne, mais d'une présence infiniment plus réelle, plus poignante, plus claire et plus pleine d'amour que cette première fois où il m'a prise. [48-49]

Sometimes the very first words [of the Lord's Prayer] tear my thought from my body and transport my thought to a place outside of space where there is neither perspective nor point of view. Space opens out. The infinity of the ordinary space of perception is replaced by an infinity to the second or sometimes to the third power. At the same time this infinity of infinity is everywhere filled with silence, not a silence that is an absence of sound. It is the object of a positive sensation, more positive than that of sound. Noise, if there is any, reaches me only after having passed through this silence. Sometimes during this recitation or at other moments Christ is present in person. But this presence is infinitely more real, more heart piercing, more luminous, and more full of love than that first time when he took hold of me.

[R]ien parmi les choses humaines n'est aussi puissant, pour maintenir le regard appliqué toujours plus intensément sur Dieu, que l'amitié pour les amis de Dieu. [51]

Among things in the human sphere nothing is more powerful for keeping the eye ever more intensely fixed on God than friendship for the friends of God.

L'incarnation du christianisme implique une solution harmonieuse du problème des relations entre individus et collectivité. Harmonie au sens pythagoricien; juste équilibre des contraires. Cette solution est ce dont les hommes ont soif précisément aujourd'hui. [55]

The concrete realization of Christianity implies a harmonious solution to the problem of the relationship between the individual and the collective. Harmony in the Pythagorean sense: the harmonious coincidence of opposites. This solution is precisely what men are thirsting for today.[6]

---

[6] Pythagoras of Samos, c. 570 – c. 495 BC, was a Greek philosopher and mathematician, and founder of the system of thought named after him.

La fonction propre de l'intelligence exige une liberté totale, impliquant le droit de tout nier, et aucune domination. Partout où elle usurpe un commandement, il y a un excès d'individualisme. Partout où elle est mal à l'aise, il y a une collectivité oppressive, ou plusieurs. [56]

Complete freedom is required if the mind is to function properly. This implies the right to reject everything, including any kind of domination. Wherever the mind usurps a commandment there is an excess of individualism. Wherever the mind is ill at ease there is an oppressive collectivity, or perhaps several of them.

Une collectivité est gardienne du dogme; et le dogme est un objet de contemplation pour l'amour, la foi et l'intelligence, trois facultés strictement individuelles. D'où un malaise de l'individu dans le christianisme, presque depuis l'origine, et notamment un malaise de l'intelligence. On ne peut le nier. [57]

The guardian of dogma is a collectivity.[7] But dogma is an object of contemplation for love, faith, and intellect, three strictly individual faculties. This explains the uneasiness of the individual in Christianity almost from its beginnings, particularly in the realm of intellect. This cannot be denied.

---

[7] The "collectivity" here is the church.

[P]ar une de ces lois de la nature que Dieu lui-même respecte, du fait qu'il les veut de toute éternité, il y a deux langages tout à fait distincts, quoique composés des même mots, le langage collectif et le langage individuel. Le Consolateur que le Christ nous envoie, l'Esprit de vérité, parle selon l'occasion l'un ou l'autre langage, et par nécessité de nature il n'y a pas concordance.

[L]e langage de la place publique n'est pas celui de la chambre nuptiale. [57-58]

By one of those natural laws that God himself respects because of the fact that he wills them from all eternity, there are two completely distinct languages, although composed of the same words: the language of the collective and the language of the individual. The Comforter, the Spirit of truth whom Christ sends us, speaks one or the other language according to circumstance. By a necessity of nature they are not in agreement.

The language of the public square is not the language of the bridal chamber.

Tout le monde sait qu'il n'y a de conversation vraiment intime qu'à deux ou trois. Déjà si l'on est cinq ou six le langage collectif commence à dominer. C'est pourquoi quand on applique à l'église la parole « Partout où deux ou trois d'entre vous seront réunis en mon nom, je serai au milieu d'eux », on commet un complet contresens. Le Christ n'a pas dit deux cents, ou cinquante, ou dix. Il a dit deux ou trois. Il a dit exactement qu'il est toujours en tiers dans l'intimité d'une amitié chrétienne, l'intimité du tête-à-tête. [58]

Everyone knows that genuinely intimate conversation is limited to two or three. Collective language begins to dominate when there are as few as five or six. This is why the application to the church of the verse — "Wherever two or three are gathered in my name, I will be in their midst"[8] — is a complete misinterpretation. Christ did not say two hundred or fifty or ten. He said two or three. He said in fact that he is always the third member in the intimacy of a Christian friendship, in the intimacy of intimate conversation.

---

[8] Matthew 18.20.

[S]i on revoit un être très cher après une longue absence, les mots qu'on échange avec lui n'importent pas, mais seulement le son de sa voix qui nous assure de sa présence. [70]

If after a long absence we see someone again — someone very dear — the words that are exchanged with him do not matter. What matters is only the sound of his voice assuring us of his presence.

Je crois qu'excepté vous, tous les êtres humains à qui il m'est jamais arrivé de donner, par mon amitié, le pouvoir de me faire facilement de la peine se sont parfois amusés à m'en faire, fréquemment ou rarement, consciemment ou inconsciemment, mais tous quelquefois. Là où je reconnaissais que c'était conscient, je prenais un couteau et je coupais l'amitié, sans d'ailleurs prévenir l'intéressé. Ils ne se conduisaient pas ainsi par méchanceté, mais par l'effet du phénomène bien connu qui pousse les poules, quand elles voient une poule blessée parmi elles, à se jeter dessus à coups de bec. [73]

I believe that other than you every human being to whom, because of friendship, I have given the power to easily hurt me have at times amused themselves by doing so. Frequently or rarely, consciously or unconsciously; but everyone at one time or another. Whenever I realized that this was conscious I took a knife and severed the friendship without even warning the individual involved. They did not act this way out of malice but because of the well-known phenomenon that makes chickens, when they see one of their number wounded, throw themselves upon the wounded chicken all the while pecking it.

Vous pouvez croire aussi sur ma parole que la Grèce, l'Égypte, l'Inde antique, la Chine antique, la beauté du monde, les reflets purs et authentiques de cette beauté dans les arts et dans la science, le spectacle des replis du cœur humain dans les cœurs vides de croyance religieuse, toutes ces choses ont fait autant que les choses visiblement chrétiennes pour me livrer captive au Christ. [76]

On my word you can believe that Greece, Egypt, ancient India, ancient China, the beauty of the world, the pure and authentic reflections of this beauty in the arts and in science, the vision of what lies in the recesses of the human heart, including in hearts devoid of religious belief; all these things have done as much as the things ostensibly Christian to make me a captive to Christ.

Les enfants de Dieu ne doivent avoir aucune autre patrie ici-bas que l'univers lui-même, avec la totalité des créatures raisonnables qu'il a contenues, contient et contiendra. C'est là la cité natale qui a droit à notre amour. [79]

The children of God should not have any other country here below than the universe itself, together with the sum of all rational creatures it has contained, does contain, and will contain. That is the native city that has the right to our love.

Nous vivons une époque tout à fait sans précédent, et dans la situation présente l'universalité, qui pouvait autrefois être implicite, doit être maintenant pleinement explicite. Elle doit imprégner le langage et toute la manière d'être. [81]

We are living in an era completely without precedent. In the present situation universality which formerly could be implicit now has to be fully explicit. It has to impregnate our language and our whole way of being.

C'est une grande douleur pour moi de craindre que les pensées qui sont descendues en moi ne soient condamnées à mort par la contagion de mon insuffisance et de ma misère [...] Mais qui sait si celles qui sont en moi ne sont pas au moins partiellement destinées à ce que vous en fassiez quelque usage? Elles ne peuvent être destinées qu'à quelqu'un qui ait un peu d'amitié pour moi, et d'amitié véritable. Car pour les autres, en quelque sorte, je n'existe pas. Je suis couleur feuille morte, comme certains insectes. [83-84]

I am stung with grief when it occurs to me that the thoughts that I have received might be condemned to death because they may be tainted by my insufficiency and my wretchedness [...] But who knows if these thoughts are not at least partially destined for whatever use you may make of them? They can be destined only for someone who might feel a little friendship toward me, but true friendship. For the others, in some sense, I do not exist. Like certain insects, I am the color of a dead leaf.

Réflexions sur le bon usage des études scolaires en vue de l'Amour de Dieu[9]

Bien qu'aujourd'hui on semble l'ignorer, la formation de la faculté d'attention est le but véritable et presque l'unique intérêt des études. La plupart des exercices scolaires ont aussi un certain intérêt intrinsèque; mais cet intérêt est secondaire. Tous les exercices qui font vraiment appel au pouvoir d'attention sont intéressants au même titre et presque également. [85-86]

---

[9] *Attente de Dieu*, pp. 85-97.

Reflections on the Good Use of School Studies
as a Path to the Love of God

Although it seems to be unknown today, the real purpose and almost the only significance of study is the formation of the faculty of attention. Most school exercises have their own intrinsic significance; but this significance is secondary. All exercises that make a genuine appeal to the faculty of attention are significant for the same reason, and almost equally

Le meilleur soutien de la foi est la garantie que si l'on demande à son Père du pain, il ne donne pas des pierres. En dehors même de toute croyance religieuse explicite, toutes les fois qu'un être humain accomplit un effort d'attention avec le seul désir de devenir plus apte à saisir la vérité, il acquiert cette aptitude plus grande, même si son effort n'a produit aucun fruit visible. [87-88]

The best support for such faith is the guarantee that if bread is asked of the Father, he does not give stones.[10] Even outside of any explicit religious belief, every time a human being succeeds in attending, with the sole desire to become more capable of grasping the truth, he acquires this capability on a larger scale, even if his effort produces no visible fruit.[11]

---

[10] Luke 11:11.

[11] Weil expands the idea of attending for the sake of coming to a love for God to the broader notion of attending for the sake of coming to a love for the truth, and this for those for whom faith in God is weak or lacking altogether.

[L]e désir, orienté vers Dieu, est la seule force capable de faire monter l'âme. Ou plutôt c'est Dieu seul qui vient saisir l'âme et la lève, mais le désir seul oblige Dieu à descendre. Il ne vient qu'à ceux qui lui demandent de venir; et ceux qui demandent souvent, longtemps, ardemment, Il ne peut pas s'empêcher de descendre vers eux. [91-92]

[D]esire, oriented toward God, is the only power able to make the soul rise up. Or rather, it is God alone who comes to take the soul and lift it up. But desire alone obliges him to come down. He comes only to those who ask him to come. And he cannot restrain himself from coming to those who ask frequently, patiently, passionately.

Il y a quelque chose dans notre âme qui répugne à la véritable attention beaucoup plus violemment que la chair ne répugne à la fatigue. Ce quelque chose est beaucoup plus proche du mal que la chair. C'est pourquoi toutes les fois qu'on fait vraiment attention, on détruit du mal en soi. Si on fait attention avec cette intention, un quart d'heure d'attention vaut beaucoup de bonnes œuvres. [92]

There is something in our soul that looks for ways to avoid genuine attention much more violently than the flesh looks for ways to avoid fatigue. This something is much closer to evil than is the flesh. This is why we destroy evil in ourselves every time we truly pay attention. If we pay attention intending such destruction, a quarter hour of attention possesses the value of many good deeds.

L'attention consiste à suspendre sa pensée, à la laisser disponible, vide et pénétrable à l'objet, à maintenir en soi-même à proximité de la pensée, mais à un niveau inférieur et sans contact avec elle, les diverses connaissances acquises qu'on est forcé d'utiliser. La pensée doit être, à toutes les pensées particulières et déjà formées, comme un homme sur une montagne qui, regardant devant lui, aperçoit en même temps sous lui, mais sans les regarder, beaucoup de forêts et de plaines. Et surtout la pensée doit être vide, en attente, ne rien chercher, mais être prête à recevoir dans sa vérité nue l'objet qui va y pénétrer. [92-93]

Attention consists in suspending the active use of the mind, leaving it available, empty, and penetrable to the object; it consists in keeping checked within ourselves, in proximity to the mind, but at a lower level and without contact with it, the varied knowledge we have acquired and which we are forced to use. In relation to particular, previously formed thoughts, the mind should be like a man on a mountain who, looking straight ahead, simultaneously sees many forests and plains below, but does not look at them. The mind should especially be empty, waiting, seeking nothing, but ready to receive the object — in its naked truth — that is coming to penetrate it.

Les biens les plus précieux ne doivent pas être cherchés, mais attendus. Car l'homme ne peut pas les trouver par ses propres forces, et s'il se met à leur recherche, il trouvera à la place des faux biens dont il ne saura pas discerner la fausseté. [93]

Good things — the most precious of them — should not be sought; they should be awaited. For man is unable to find them by his own powers. If he sets out to look for them, he will find imitations in their place. And he will be unable to discern that they are imitations.

Ce n'est pas seulement l'amour de Dieu qui a pour substance l'attention. L'amour du prochain, dont nous savons que c'est le même amour, est fait de la même substance. Les malheureux n'ont pas besoin d'autre chose en ce monde que d'hommes capables de faire attention à eux. La capacité de faire attention à un malheureux est chose très rare, très difficile; c'est presque un miracle; c'est un miracle. [96]

Attention is not only the very substance of love for God. Love for our neighbor, which we know to be the same love, is made of the same substance. Those who suffer have need of nothing else in this world than of people who are capable of paying attention to them. The capacity to pay attention to such a person is something very rare, very difficult; it is almost a miracle; it *is* a miracle.

Dans la première légende du Graal, il est dit que le Graal, pierre miraculeuse qui par la vertu de l'hostie consacrée rassasie toute faim, appartient à quiconque dira le premier au gardien de la pierre, roi trois quarts paralysé par la plus douloureuse blessure: « Quel est ton tourment? »   [96]

In the first Grail legend it is said that the Grail, a miraculous stone satisfying all hunger because of the consecrated host, belongs to whomever is the first to say to the stone's guardian, a king three-quarters paralyzed by the most painful of wounds, these words: *What is it that you are going through?*

La plénitude de l'amour du prochain, c'est simplement d'être capable de lui demander: « Quel est ton tourment? » C'est savoir que le malheureux existe, non pas comme un exemplaire de la catégorie sociale étiqueté « malheureux », mais en tant qu'homme, exactement semblable à nous, qui a été un jour frappé et marqué d'une marque inimitable par le malheur. Pour cela il est suffisant, mais indispensable, de savoir poser sur lui un certain regard.

Ce regard est d'abord un regard attentif, où l'âme se vide de tout contenu propre pour recevoir en elle-même l'être qu'elle regarde tel qu'il est, dans toute sa vérité. Seul en est capable celui qui est capable d'attention. [96-97]

The fullness of love for neighbor consists simply in being capable of asking him: *What is it that you are going through?* This is an acknowledgement that the one suffering exists not as a specimen of the social category labeled "afflicted," but as a human being just like us who one day was struck, branded with a mark like no other. For this it is enough — but it is indispensable — to know how to look upon him.

This look is first of all an attentive look, a look by means of which the soul is emptied of all its own content in order to receive within itself the one looked upon exactly as he is, in the whole truth of his condition. Only the person capable of attention is capable of doing this.

Formes de l'Amour implicite de Dieu[12]

Une certaine réciprocité est essentielle à l'amitié. Si d'un des deux cotés toute bienveillance est entièrement absente, l'autre doit supprimer l'affection en lui-même par respect pour le libre consentement auquel il ne doit pas désirer porter atteinte. Si d'un des deux cotés il n'y a pas respect pour l'autonomie de l'autre, celui-ci doit couper le lien par respect de soi-même. [203]

---

[12] *Attente de Dieu*, pp. 122-214,

Forms of Implicit Love for God

Essential to friendship is a certain reciprocity. If unqualified willingness is lacking on the part of one, the other has to suppress his own affection out of respect for that person's free consent which he must never even wish to compromise. If respect for the autonomy of the other is lacking on the part of one, the other has to sever the bond out of respect for himself.

L'amitié est le miracle par lequel un être humain accepte de regarder à distance et sans s'approcher l'être même qui lui est nécessaire comme une nourriture. [204]

Friendship is the miracle by which a human being accepts looking from a distance, without encroaching, upon the very being who is as necessary to him as food.

Love by George Herbert [13]

Love bade me welcome; yet my soul drew back,
Guiltie of dust and sinne.
But quick-ey'd Love, observing me grow slack
From my first entrance in,
Drew nearer to me, sweet questioning,
If I lacked any thing.

A guest, I answer'd, worthy to be here:
Love said, You shall be he.
I, the unkinde, ungratefull? Ah my deare,
I cannot look on thee.
Love took my hand, and smiling did reply,
Who made the eyes but I?

Truth Lord, but I have marr'd them: let my shame
Go where it doth deserve.
And know you not, sayes Love,
   who bore the blame?
My deare, then I will serve.
You must sit down, sayes Love,
   and taste my meat:
So I did sit and eat.

---

[13] *The Complete Poems of George Herbert*, p. 178.

Écrits de Londres
London Writings

Profession de Foi[14]

Il est une réalité situé hors du monde, c'est-à-dire hors de l'espace et du temps, hors de l'univers mental de l'homme, hors de tout le domaine que les facultés humaines peuvent atteindre.

A cette réalité répond au centre du cœur de l'homme cette exigence d'un bien absolu qui y habite toujours et ne trouve jamais aucun objet en ce monde.

Elle est aussi rendue manifeste ici-bas par les absurdités, les contradictions insolubles, auxquelles se heurte toujours la pensée humaine quand elle se meut seulement en ce monde.

De même que la réalité de ce monde-ci est l'unique fondement des faits, de meme l'autre réalité est l'unique fondement du Bien.

C'est d'elle uniquement que descend en ce monde tout le bien susceptible d'y exister, toute beauté, toute verité, toute justice, toute légitimé, tout ordre, toute subordination de la conduite humaine à des obligations.

L'unique intermédiaire par lequel le bien puisse descendre de chez elle au milieu des hommes, ce sont ceux qui parmi les hommes ont leur attention et leur amour tournés vers elle.

---

[14] *Écrits de Londres*, pp. 74-75.

Profession of Faith

There is a Reality that exists beyond this world, that is, beyond space and time, beyond the scope of human thought, and beyond the grasp of every human faculty.

To this Reality corresponds, at the center of the human heart, the need for an absolute Good which is always there, and which never finds an object in this world.

This need is also manifested here below by the absurdities, the insoluble contradictions with which human thought always collides when it moves solely in this world.

Just as the reality of this world is the sole foundation of facts, so also that other Reality is the sole foundation of the Good.

All the good that can possibly exist, all beauty, all truth, all justice, all things permitted, all order, all subordination of human conduct to duty: All of this comes into the world solely from this Reality.

The only intermediaries by which the Good can descend from its dwelling to the place where men live are those human beings who have their attention and their love turned toward the Good.

Cette Guerre est une guerre de religions[15]

L'école sociologique française a presque raison dans son explication sociale de la religion. Il s'en faut d'un infiniment petit qu'elle ait raison. Seulement cet infiniment petit est le grain de sénevé, la perle dans le champ, le levain dans la pâte, le sel dans la nourriture. Cet infiniment petit est Dieu, c'est-à-dire infiniment plus que tout. [103]

---

[15] *Écrits de Londres*, pp. 98-103.

This is a Religious War

The French School of sociology is almost correct in its social explanation of religion. Except for an infinitely tiny bit it would be correct. But this infinitely tiny bit is the mustard seed, the pearl in the field, the leaven in dough, the salt in food. This infinitely tiny bit is God, which is to say, infinitely more than everything.

Dans la vie d'un people comme dans la vie d'une âme, il s'agit seulement de mettre cet infiniment petit au centre. [103]

In the life of a people as in the life of a soul, it is only a matter of placing this infinitely tiny bit at the center.

Fragments et Notes

L'histoire est basée sur la documentation, c'est-à-dire sur le temoignage des meurtriers concernant les victims. [157]

Fragments and Notes

History is based on documentation, which is to say, on the testimony of murderers concerning their victims.

Le critérium de l'arbre et ses fruits est par avance la condamnation de la notion d'orthodoxie. [159]

The criterion of the tree and its fruits[16] condemns in advance the notion of orthodoxy.

---

[16] Cf. Matthew 5.15-20.

La science est un effort pour apercevoir l'ordonn-nance de l'univers. Par suite c'est un contact de la pensée humaine avec la sagesse éternelle. C'est quelque chose comme un sacrement. [159]

Science is an effort to perceive the order of the universe. It is consequently a contact between human thought and eternal wisdom. It is something like a sacrament.

Qu'est-ce que la culture? Formation de l'attention. Participation aux trésors de spiritualité et de poésie accumulés par l'humanité au cours des ages. Connaissance de l'homme. Connaissance concrete du bien et du mal. [160]

What is culture? The formation of attention. The participation in the treasures of spirituality and poetry accumulated by humanity in the course of the ages. The knowledge of man. The concrete knowledge of good and evil.

Dieu vient à l'âme dépouillé de toute splendeur. Il vient seulement comme quelque chose qui demande à être aimé. [166]

God, stripped of all splendor, comes to the soul. He comes only as something that asks to be loved.

Lettre à un religieux
Letter to a Priest

From Lettre à un religieux New York 1942

Quand je lis le catéchisme du Concile de Trente, il me semble n'avoir rien de commun avec la religion qui est y exposée. Quand je lis le Nouveau Testament, les mystiques, la liturgie, quand je vois célébrer la messe, je sens avec une espèce de certitude que cette foi est la mienne, ou plus exactement serait la mienne sans la distance mise entre elle et moi par mon imperfection. Cela fait une situation spirituelle pénible. Je voudrais la rendre, non pas moins pénible, mais plus claire. N'importe quelle peine est acceptable dans la clarté. [11]

From A Letter to a Priest New York 1942

When I read the catechism of the Council of Trent,[17] it seems to me to have nothing in common with the religion that is set out in it. When I read the New Testament, the mystics, the liturgy, when I see the Mass being celebrated, I feel with a kind of certitude that this faith is mine or, more precisely, that it would be mine without the distance placed between it and me by my imperfection. This makes for a painful spiritual situation. I would like to make it not less painful but more clear. No matter what the pain, it is acceptable provided there is clarity.

---

[17] This council opened at Trent in December 1545 and closed there in December 1563. It was called to deal with the challenges posed by the Reformation.

Je pense à ces choses depuis des années avec toute l'intensité d'amour et d'attention dont je dispose. Cette intensité est misérablement faible, à cause de mon imperfection qui est très grande; mais elle va toujours en croissant, il me semble. À mesure qu'elle croît, les liens qui m'attachent à la foi catholique deviennent de plus en plus forts, de plus en plus profondément enracinés dans le cœur et l'intelligence. Mais en même temps les pensées qui m'éloignent de l'église gagnent elles aussi en force et en clarté. Si ces pensées sont vraiment incompatible avec l'appartenance à l'Église, il n'a donc guère d'espoir que je puisse jamais avoir part aux sacrements. S'il en est ainsi, je ne vois pas comment je peux éviter de conclure que j'ai pour vocation d'être chrétienne hors de l'église. [13-14]

For years I have been intensely thinking about these things with all the love and attention at my disposal. Although miserably weak because of my considerable imperfection, this intensity is continually increasing, or so it seems to me. To the extent that it is increasing, the ties which bind me to the Catholic faith are becoming more and more powerful, more and more deeply rooted in my heart and mind. However, at the same time the thoughts which distance me from the church are also gaining in strength and in clarity. If these thoughts are genuinely incompatible with membership in the church there is hardly any hope that I could ever take part in the sacraments. If this turns out to be the case, I don't see how I can avoid concluding that my vocation is to be a Christian outside of the church.

Les opinions qui suivent ont pour moi des degrés divers de probabilité ou de certitude mais toutes sont accompagnées dans mon esprit d'un point d'interrogation. Je ne les exprimerai à l'indicatif qu'à cause de la pauvreté du langage; j'aurais besoin que la conjugaison contienne un mode supplémentaire. Dans le domaine des choses saintes, je n'affirme rien catégoriquement. Mais celles de mes opinions qui sont conformes à l'enseignement de l'église sont aussi acompagnées dans mon esprit du même point d'interrogation. [14-15]

The opinions which follow possess for me different degrees of probability or of certitude. But in my mind all of them are accompanied by a question mark. I will express them in the indicative mood only because of the poverty of language; what is needed is a supplementary grammatical mood. In the domain of the sacred I affirm nothing categorically. At the same time, such of my opinions that are compatible with the teaching of the church are accompanied in my mind by the same question mark.

Je considère une certaine suspension du jugement à l'égard de toutes les pensées quelque qu'elles soient, sans exception, comme constituant la vertu d'humilité dans le domaine de l'intelligence. [15]

In regard to all thoughts, whatever they might be and without exception, I consider that withholding judgment constitutes the virtue of humility in the intellectual realm.

Ce que nous nommons idolâtrie est dans une large mesure une fiction [...] Tous les peuples de tous les temps ont toujours été monothéistes. [17]

What we call idolatry is to a large extent a fiction [...] All peoples at all times have always been monotheists.

Si la Rédemption, avec les signes et les moyens sensibles qui lui correspondent, n'avait pas été présente sur terre depuis l'origine, on ne pourrait pas pardonner à Dieu — s'il est permis d'employer ces mots sans blasphème — le malheur de tant d'innocents, déracinés, asservis, torturés et mis à mort au cours des siècles antérieurs à l'ère chrétienne. Le Christ est présent sur cette terre, à moins que les hommes ne le chassent, partout où il y a crime et malheur. Sans les effets surnaturels de cette présence, comment les innocents écrasés par le malheur éviteraient-ils de tomber dans le crime de maudire Dieu, et par suite dans la damnation? [20]

If redemption, together with the outward signs and means which correspond to it, had not been present on the earth from the beginning, we could not forgive God — if such words can be used without blasphemy — for the affliction of so many innocent people who have been uprooted, subjugated, tortured, and put to death in the course of the centuries prior to the Christian era. Christ is present on this earth, at least to the extent that men do not chase him away, wherever there is crime and suffering. Without the supernatural effects of this presence, how would the innocent, crushed by affliction, avoid falling into the crime of cursing God and consequently into damnation?

Pour que le christianisme s'incarne vraiment, pour que l'inspiration chrétienne imprègne la vie tout entière, il faut reconnaître au préalable qu'historiquement notre civilisation profane procède d'une inspiration religieuse qui, bien que chronologiquement pré-chrétiennes, était chrétienne en son essence. La Sagesse de Dieu doit être regardée comme la source unique de toute lumière ici-bas. [23]

In order for Christianity truly to be incarnated, in order for Christian inspiration to impregnate all of life, it must first be recognized that historically our secular civilization emanates from a religious inspiration which, although chronologically pre-Christian, was Christian in its essence. The wisdom of God must be regarded as the only source of all light here below.

Si le poème scandinave *La Rune d'Odin* est antérieur à toute contamination chrétienne (ce qui est invérifiable), il contient aussi une prophétie très frappante: « Je sais que j'ai pendu à un arbre balancé par le vent, neuf nuits entières, blessé d'une lance, offert à Odin, moi-même à moi-même. A cet arbre dont nul ne sait de quelle racine il sort. Nul ne m'a donné du pain, ni une corne pour boire. J'ai regardé en bas, je me suis appliqué aux runes, en pleurant je les ai appris, puis je suis descendu de là. » (Première Edda) [25-26]

If the Scandinavian poem *The Rune of* Odin[18] is prior to any Christian corruption (which is unverifiable), it too contains a prophecy that is quite striking: "I know that for nine whole nights I hung upon a tree upon which the wind beat. I was wounded by a spear. I was offered to Odin. Myself to myself. On this tree, sprung from a root no one knows. No one gave me bread, nor a cup in order to drink. I looked below. I applied myself to the runes and, weeping, I learned them. Then I descended from that tree" (First Edda).

---

[18] The runes were said to be a gift from the Norse god Odin (or Woden). They were seen as symbols of authority; the word *Rune* means *Mystery*. Odin, the principal Scandinavian god, hung upon the world tree, Yggdrasil, for nine days and nights; he did this so that he could acquire knowledge held by the runes. When he saw them below him, he took them up and so received their power.

Comme le disent les Hindous, Dieu est à la fois personnel et impersonnel. Il est impersonnel en ce sens que sa manière infiniment mystérieuse d'être une Personne diffère infiniment de la manière humaine. On ne peut pas saisir ce mystère qu'en employant à la fois, comme deux pinces, ces deux notions contraires, incompatibles ici-bas, compatibles seulement en Dieu. [39-40]

As the Hindus say, God is at the same time personal and impersonal. He is impersonal in the sense that his infinitely mysterious way of being a Person differs infinitely from the way in which a human being is a person. This mystery can be grasped only by employing at the same time, like two pincers, these two contrary notions, incompatible here below, compatible only in God.

Des saints d'une très haute spiritualité, comme Saint Jean de la Croix, ont saisi simultanément et avec une force égale l'aspect personnel et l'aspect impersonnel de Dieu. Des âmes moins avancées portent leur attention et leur foi surtout ou exclusivement sur l'un de ces deux aspects. [40-41]

Saints of a very high spirituality, such as Saint John of the Cross, have grasped — simultaneously and with an equal force — the personal aspect and the impersonal aspect of God. Less advanced souls give their attention and their faith especially or exclusively to one of these two aspects.

[U]n athée, un « infidèle », capables de compassion pure sont aussi proches de Dieu qu'un chrétien, et par suite le connaissent aussi bien, bien que leur connaissance s'exprime par d'autres paroles, ou reste meutte. Car « Dieu est Amour ». Et s'il rétribue ceux qui le cherchent, il donne la lumière à ceux qui l'approchent, surtout s'ils désirent la lumière. [43]

Atheists and "infidels" who are capable of pure compassion are as near to God as a Christian and therefore they know him just as well, although their knowledge is expressed with other words or with none at all. For "God is Love."[19] And if he rewards those who seek him,[20] he gives light to those who draw near to him,[21] especially if they desire light.

---

[19] I John 4.16.
[20] Hebrews 11.6.
[21] Cf. James 4.8; also Hebrews 7.19, Psalm 69.18.

La conception thomiste de la foi implique un « totalitarisme » aussi étouffant ou davantage que celui de Hitler. Car si l'esprit adhère complètement, non seulement à tout ce que l'église a reconnu comme étant de foi stricte, mais encore à tout ce qu'elle reconnaîtra jamais comme tel, l'intelligence doit être bâillonnée et réduite à des tâches serviles. [44-45]

The Thomist conception of the faith[22] implies a "totalitarianism," as suffocating or even more so than that of Hitler. For if the mind completely adheres not only to everything that the church *has* recognized as obligatory, but even to everything that it *will* recognize as such, the intellect has to be gagged and reduced to servility.

---

[22] The position held and taught by Thomas Aquinas (1225-1274), whose formula, as cited by Weil in this letter, is: "Whoever refuses to accept one single article of the Faith does not possess the Faith to any degree."

La métaphore de « voile » ou de « reflet » appliquée par les mystiques à la foi leur permet de sortir de cet étouffoir. Ils acceptent l'enseignement de l'église, non pas comme étant la vérité, mais comme étant quelque chose derrière quoi on trouve la vérité. [45]

The metaphor "veil" or "reflection," applied by the mystics to dogma, allows them to escape from this suffocation. They accept the teaching of the church not as the truth but as something behind which the truth is found.

Les dogmes de la foi ne sont pas des choses à affirmer. Ce sont des choses à regarder à une certaine distance, avec attention, respect et amour. C'est le serpent d'airain dont la vertu est telle que quiconque le regarde vivra. Ce regard attentif et aimant, par un choc en retour, fait jaillir dans l'âme une source de lumière qui illumine tous les aspects de la vie humaine ici-bas. Les dogmes perdent cette vertu dès qu'on les affirme. [54]

The dogmas of the faith are not things to affirm. They are things to look upon from a certain distance with attention, respect, and love. Like the bronze serpent whose power is such that whoever looks upon it will live.[23] This attentive and loving look, returning to the onlooker, becomes a source of light bursting forth in the soul and illumining every aspect of human life here below. Dogmas lose this power as soon as they are affirmed.

---

[23] Numbers 21.5-9.

Les mystères de la foi ne sont pas un objet pour l'intelligence en tant que faculté qui permet d'affirmer ou de nier. Ils ne sont pas de l'ordre de la vérité, mais au-dessus. La seule partie de l'âme humaine qui soit capable d'un contact réel avec eux, c'est la faculté d'amour surnaturel. [64-65]

The mysteries of the faith are not objects for the intellect insofar as it is the faculty of affirmation or denial. They are not of the order of truth, but above that. The only part of the human soul which may be capable of real contact with them is the faculty of supernatural love.

La vertu de charité est l'exercice de la faculté d'amour surnaturel. La vertu de foi est la subordination de toutes les facultés de l'âme à la faculté d'amour surnaturel. La vertu d'espérance est une orientation de l'âme vers une transformation après laquelle elle sera tout entière et exclusivement amour. [65]

The virtue of charity is the exercise of the faculty of supernatural love. The virtue of faith is the subordination of all the faculties of the soul to the faculty of supernatural love. The virtue of hope is an orientation of the soul toward a transformation after which it will be wholly and exclusively love.

Quand l'intelligence, ayant fait silence pour laisser l'amour envahir toute l'âme, recommence de nouveau à s'exercer, elle se trouve contenir davantage de lumière qu'auparavant, davantage d'aptitude à saisir les objets, les vérités qui lui sont propres. Bien plus, je crois que ces silences constituent pour elle une éducation qui ne peut avoir aucun autre équivalent et lui permettent de saisir des vérités qui autrement lui resteraient toujours cachées. Il y a des vérités qui sont à sa portée, saisissables pour elle, mais qu'elle ne peut saisir qu'après avoir passé en silence à travers l'inintelligible. [66]

When the intellect, after stilling itself in order to allow love to invade the whole soul, begins to exercise itself again, it is found to contain more light than before, more aptitude to grasp things, to lay hold of the truths which are proper to it. Even more, I believe that silence constitutes for the intellect an education which can have no other equivalent and which permits it to grasp truths which otherwise would remain forever hidden from it. There are truths that are within its capability, graspable by it, but which it can only grasp after having passed in silence through the unintelligible.

Le premier silence, long d'un instant à peine, qui se produit à travers toute l'âme en faveur de l'amour surnaturel, c'est le grain jeté par le Semeur, c'est la graine de sénevé presque invisible qui deviendra un jour l'Arbre de la Croix. [67]

The initial silence, hardly an instant long, spreading throughout the soul for the sake of supernatural love, is the seed sown by the Sower,[24] the barely visible mustard seed[25] which one day will become the Tree of the Cross.

---

[24] Matthew 13.3-8.
[25] Matthew 13.31-32.

[Q]uand on fait parfaitement attention à une musique parfaitement belle (et de même pour l'architecture, la peinture, etc.), l'intelligence n'y trouve rien à affirmer ou à nier. Mais toutes les facultés de l'âme, y compris l'intelligence, font silence et sont suspendues à l'audition. L'audition est appliquée à un objet incompréhensible, mais qui enferme de la réalité et du bien. Et l'intelligence, qui n'y saisit aucune vérité, y trouve néanmoins une nourriture. [67]

When we have paid perfect attention to a perfectly beautiful piece of music (and the same is true for architecture, painting, etc.), the intellect finds nothing there to affirm or deny. But all the faculties of the soul, including the intellect, are silent and their use suspended for the sake of hearing. Hearing is applied to an object that is not meant to be comprehended, but which contains what is both real and good. And the intellect, although grasping no truth there, nevertheless finds nourishment in it.[26]

---

[26] "The volatile truth of our words should continually betray the inadequacy of the residual statement. Their truth is *instantly* translated; its literal monument alone remains. The words which express our faith and piety are not definite; yet they are significant and fragrant like frankincense to superior natures." Henry David Thoreau, *Walden.*

L'adhésion de l'intelligence [...] n'est jamais à aucun degré chose volontaire. L'attention seule est volontaire. Aussi est-elle *seule* matière d'obligation. Si on veut provoquer en soi volontairement une adhésion de l'intelligence, c'est la suggestion. [68]

Intellectual assent [...] never involves the will. Only attention can be willed. And it alone is a matter of obligation. If one wishes to will intellectual assent into existence, this is auto-suggestion.

On pourrait poser en postulat: Est fausse toute conception de Dieu incompatible avec un mouvement de charité pure. [72]

The following could be proposed as a postulate: Every conception of God that is incompatible with pure love is false.

L'amour et la connaissance de Dieu ne sont pas réellement séparables. [72]

In reality love and the knowledge of God are not separable.

La parole « Soyez parfaits comme votre Père céleste est parfait », venant aussitôt après « Votre Père, celui des cieux, fait lever son soleil sur les mauvais et les bons et fait pleuvoir sur les injustes et les justes » implique toute une doctrine, qui à ma connaissance n'est développée nulle part. Car le Christ cite comme trait suprême de la justice de Dieu ce qu'on allègue toujours (exemple Job) pour l'accuser d'injustice, à savoir qu'il favorise indifféremment les bons et les mauvais. [76-77]

The saying, "Be perfect as your heavenly Father is perfect,"[27] coming immediately after, "Your heavenly Father makes the sun rise on the bad and the good, and makes the rain fall on the unjust and the just,"[28] implies a complete doctrine which, to my knowledge, is nowhere developed. For Christ cites as the supreme mark of God's justice what is always alleged (for example, Job) in order to accuse him of injustice, namely, that he favors the good and the bad indifferently.

---

[27] Matthew 5.48.
[28] Matthew 5.45.

De plus cette lumière et cette eau ont probablement aussi une signification spirituelle, c'est-à-dire que tous — dans Israël et dehors, dans l'église et dehors — sont *egalement* inondés de grâce, bien que la plupart la refusent. [77]

Moreover, this light and this water probably have a spiritual significance as well, namely, that everyone — in and out of Israel, in and out of the church — is *equally* inundated with grace, although the majority rejects it.

[L'impartialité divine] est tout à fait contraire à la conception courante selon laquelle Dieu envoie arbitrairement plus de grâce à l'un, moins à l'autre, comme un souverain capricieux; cela sous le prétexte qu'il ne la doit pas! Il doit à sa propre bonté infinie d'accorder à chaque créature la plénitude du bien. Il faut plutôt penser qu'il répand continuellement sur chacun la plénitude de la grâce, mais on y consent plus ou moins. En matière purement spirituelle, Dieu exauce tous les désirs. Ceux qui ont moins ont moins demandé. [77-78]

[God's impartiality] is altogether contrary to the current conception according to which God, like a capricious despot, arbitrarily sends more grace to one and less to another, and that under the pretext that he owes it to no one! He owes it to his own infinite goodness to grant to every creature the fullness of good. We must rather think that he continually bestows upon each and every one the fullness of his grace but that some consent to receive more of it, some less. In purely spiritual matters, God grants all desires. Those who have less have asked for less.

La parole « Il était la lumière vraie illuminant tout homme qui vient au monde » contredit absolument la doctrine catholique du baptême. Car dès lors, le Verbe habite en secret en tout homme, baptisé ou non. [78]

The saying, "He was the true light enlightening every man who comes into the world,"[29] absolutely contradicts the Catholic doctrine of baptism. It follows from this saying that the Word dwells secretly in every man, baptized or not.

---

[29] John 1.9.

La Pesanteur et la Grâce
Gravity & Grace

Tous les mouvements *naturels* de l'âme sont régis par des lois analogues à celles de la pesanteur matérielle. La grâce seule fait exception. [7]

All the *natural* movements of the soul are governed by laws analogous to those of physical gravity. Grace is the sole exception.

Il faut toujours s'attendre à ce que les choses se passent conformément à la pesanteur, sauf intervention du surnaturel. [7]

In the absence of divine intervention, we must always expect things to happen in conformity with the laws of gravity.

Deux forces régnent sur l'univers: lumière et pesanteur. [7]

Two forces reign over the universe: light and gravity.

Pesanteur. — D'une manière générale, ce qu'on attend des autres est déterminé par les effets de la pesanteur en nous; ce qu'on en reçoit est déterminé par les effets de la pesanteur en eux. Parfois cela coïncide (par hasard), souvent non. [7]

Gravity: — Generally, what we expect from others is determined by the effects of gravity on us; what we receive from them is determined by the effects of gravity on them. Sometimes (by chance) these coincide; often they do not.

Pourquoi est-ce que dès qu'un être humain témoigne qu'il a peu ou beaucoup besoin d'un autre, celui-ci s'éloigne? Pesanteur. [7]

Why is that as soon as a person indicates he has a need, be it small or great, of someone else, the latter goes away? Gravity.

Le bas et le superficiel sont au même niveau. « Il aime violemment mais bassement » : phrase possible. «Il aime profondément mais bassement »: phrase impossible. [8]

What is base and what is superficial are on the same level. "He loves violently, but basely": a possible statement. "He loves deeply, but basely": an impossible statement.

Ne pas juger. Toutes les fautes sont égales. [10]

Do not judge. All faults are equal.

Il n'y a qu'une faute: ne pas avoir la capacité de nourrir de lumière. Car cette capacité étant abolie, toutes les fautes sont possibles. [10]

There is only one fault: not to have the capacity to be nourished with the light. Once this capacity is abolished, all faults are possible.

La grâce, c'est la loi du mouvement descendant. [10]

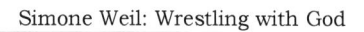

Grace, the law of descending movement.

Un malheur trop grand met un être human au-dessous de la pitié: dégoût, horreur et mépris. [10]

An affliction that is too great puts a human being beneath pity: disgust, loathing, and contempt.

Ceux qui sont tombés si bas ont-ils pitié d'eux-mêmes? [11]

Those who have fallen so low, do they have pity for themselves?

Toute forme de récompense constitue une dégradation d'énergie. [16]

Every kind of compensation constitutes a degradation of energy.

Le contentement de soi après une bonne action (ou œuvre d'art) est une dégradation d'énergie supérieure. C'est pouquoi la main droite doit ignorer... [16]

Self-satisfaction following a good act (or executing a work of art) is a degradation of energy. This is why the right hand must not know...[30]

---

[30] "Therefore when thou doest thine alms, do not sound a trumpet before thee, as the hypocrites do in the synagogues and in the streets, that they may have glory of men. Verily I say unto you, they have their reward. But when thou doest alms, let not thy left hand know what thy right hand doeth: that thine alms may be in secret: and thy Father which seeth in secret himself shall reward thee openly. " Matthew 6.2-4 KJV

La grâce comble, mais elle ne peut entrer que là où Il y a un vide pour la recevoir, et c'est elle qui fait ce vide. [18]

Grace fills, but it can only go where there is an empty place to receive it. And it is grace that creates this empty place.

Renoncer à tout ce qui n'est pas la grâce et ne pas désirer la grâce. [21]

Renounce everything that is not grace, and then do not desire grace.

Détacher notre désir de tous les biens et attendre. L'expérience prouve que cette attente est comblée. On touche alors le bien absolu. [21]

Detach our desire from all earthly goods and wait with expectation. Experience proves that this expectant waiting is satisfied. We then encounter the Absolute Good.

L'amour n'est pas consolation, il est lumière. [22]

Love is not consolation; it is light.

L'attachement est fabricateur d'illusions, et quiconque veut le réel doit être détaché. [22]

Attachment fabricates illusions. Whoever wants what is real must be detached.

Electre pleurant Oreste mort. Si on aime Dieu en pensant qu'il n'existe pas, il manifestera son existence. [24]

Electra weeping for the dead Orestes. If we love God while thinking that he does not exist, he will manifest his existence.

L'imagination travaille continuellement à boucher toutes les fissures par où passerait la grâce. [25]

The imagination works without letup to fill in all the little cracks through which grace might enter.

Le temps est une image de l'éternité, mais c'est aussi un ersatz de l'éternité. [28]

Time is an image of eternity, but it is a false image of eternity.

Reniement de saint Pierre. Dire au Christ: moi, je te resterai fidèle, c'est déjà le renier, car c'était supposer en soi et non dans la grâce la source de la fidélité. Heureusement, comme il était élu, ce reniement est devenu manifeste pour tous et pour lui. Chez combien d'autres, de telles vantardises s'accomplissent et ils ne comprennent jamais. [34]

The denial of St. Peter. To say to Christ: *I* will remain loyal to you, this is already a denial of him, for this would suppose the source of loyalty to be in oneself and not in grace. Fortunately, since he was chosen, Peter's denial became known to everyone, as well as to himself. In how many others is such boasting present and they never understand.

Supplier un homme, c'est une tentative désespérée pour faire passer à force d'intensité son propre système de valeurs dans l'esprit de l'autre. Supplier Dieu, c'est le contraire; tentative pour faire passer les valeurs divines dans sa propre âme. [34]

To supplicate a human being is a desperate attempt to transfer, by means of forceful intensity, one's own system of values into the mind of another. To supplicate God is the opposite; it is the attempt to transfer divine values into one's own soul.

Je suis tout. Mais ce « je » là est Dieu. Et ce n'est pas un « je ». [40]

I am all.[31] But here this "I" is God. And this is not an "I."

---

[31] "God is not part of the whole. God is not the whole of parts. This is what God is: undivided wholeness, unfillable fullness." Pseudo-Dionysius, *De divinis nominibus* 649C (GAB).

Le mal fait la distinction, empêche que Dieu soit équivalent à tout. [40]

Evil makes distinctions, prevents God from being equivalent to all.

Une très belle femme qui regarde son image au miroir peut très bien croire qu'elle est cela. Une femme laide sait qu'elle n'est pas cela. [43]

A very beautiful woman who looks at her image in the mirror can very well believe that she is that image. An ugly woman knows that she cannot be.

Communion catholique. Dieu ne s'est fait une fois chair, il se fait tous les jours matière pour se donner à l'homme et en être consommé. Réciproquement, par la fatigue, le malheur, la mort, l'homme est fait matière et consommé par Dieu. Comment refuser cette réciprocité? [44]

Catholic Communion. God did not make himself flesh once; he makes himself matter every day in order to give himself to man and to be consumed by him. Reciprocally, by weariness, affliction, death, man is made matter and consumed by God. How can this reciprocity be refused?[32]

---

[32] If "Love is pure [...] when you ask from God only himself" (*Cloud*, p. 238), then God, whose love by definition must always be pure, asks us only for ourselves.

Dieu n'a pu créer qu'en se cachant. Autrement il n'y aurait que lui. [49]

God could create only by hiding himself. Otherwise there would have been nothing but him.

L'humilité, c'est le refus d'exister en dehors de Dieu. Reine des vertus. [51]

Humility is the refusal to exist outside of God. The queen of virtues.

Le soleil luit sur les justes et sur les injustes [...]
Dieu se fait nécessité. Deux faces de la nécessité:
exercée et subie. Soleil et croix. [54]

The sun shines on the just and the unjust [...] God makes himself necessity. Two aspects of necessity: active and passive. Sun and cross.[33]

---

[33] "But I tell you, love your enemies and pray for those who persecute you, that you may be children of your Father in heaven. He causes his sun to rise on the evil and the good, and sends rain on the righteous and the unrighteous. If you love those who love you, what reward will you get?) Are not even the tax collectors doing that?" Matthew 5:44-46 NIV

Accepter d'être soumis à la nécessité. [54]

Accept submission to necessity.

Aimer la nécessité. [55]

Love necessity.

Veiller au niveau où on met l'infini. Si on le met au niveau où le fini seul convient, peu importe de quel nom on le nomme. [60]

Be careful at what level you place the Infinite. If you place it where the finite alone goes, it matters little what name you call it.

Les parties basses de moi-même doivent aimer Dieu, mais non pas trop. Ce ne serait pas Dieu. Qu'elles aiment comme on a soif et faim. [66-67]

My lower aspects of myself should also love God, but not too much. This would not be God. Let them love just as they hunger and thirst.

Crainte de Dieu dans saint Jean de la Croix. N'est-ce pas la crainte de penser à Dieu alors qu'on est indigne? De le souiller en le pensant mal? Par cette crainte, les parties basses s'éloignent de Dieu. [67]

Fear of God in St. John of the Cross; is it not the fear of thinking of God when one is unworthy? To taint him by thinking of him in the wrong way? By this fear the lower aspects of myself will withdraw from God.

Une science qui ne nous approche pas de Dieu ne vaut rien. Mais si elle nous en fait mal approcher, c'est-à-dire d'un Dieu imaginaire, c'est pire. [68]

A science that does not bring us to God is worth nothing. But if it brings us there in the wrong way, that is, to an imaginary god, that's worse.[34]

---

[34] "Science is the effort to discern the order of the universe. As a consequence it is a contact of human thought with eternal wisdom. It is something like a sacrament." S.W., *Écrits de Londres et dernières lettres*, p. 159.

Il faut un travail pour exprimer le vraie. Aussi pour le recevoir. On exprime et on reçoit le faux, ou du moins le superficiel, sans travail. [69]

Effort is required in order to express the truth.[35] Also in order to receive it. One expresses and one receives the false, or at least the superficial, without effort.

---

[35] "Attention is an effort, perhaps the greatest of efforts [...] However [...] there is something in our soul that looks for ways to avoid genuine attention." S.W., *Attente de Dieu*, p. 92.

Quand le vrai semble au moins aussi vrai que le faux, c'est le triomphe de la sainteté ou du génie; ainsi saint François faisait pleurer ses auditeurs tout comme un prédicateur vulgaire et théatral. [69]

When the truth seems at least as true as the false, this is the triumph of holiness or genius; thus Saint Francis[36] was making his listeners weep just like a common theatrical preacher.

---

[36] Giovanni Francesco Bernardone, 1182-1226, founder of the Order of Friars Minor (Franciscans).

Idolâtrie vient de ce qu'ayant soif de bien absolu, on ne possède pas l'attention surnaturelle et on n'a pas la patience de la laisser pousser. [72]

Idolatry comes from thirsting for the Absolute Good, but not possessing supernatural attention and not having the patience to let it blossom.

Ce n'est pas parce que Dieu nous aime que nous devons l'aimer. C'est parce que Dieu nous aime que nous devons nous aimer. [74]

It is not because God loves us that we should love him. It is because God loves us that we should love ourselves.

L'amour de Dieu est pur quand la joie and la souffrance inspirent une *égale* gratitude. [75]

Love for God is pure when joy and suffering evoke an *equal* gratitude.

Parmi les êtres humains, on ne reconnaît pleinement l'existence que de ceux qu'on aime. [76]

Human beings recognize the existence only of those they love.

La croyance à l'existence d'autres êtres humains comme tels est *amour*. [76]

Belief in the existence of other human beings as human beings is love.

Monotonie du mal: rien de nouveau; tout est *équivalent.* Rien de réel; tout est imaginaire. [82]

The monotony of evil: nothing new; everything is equivalent. Nothing real; everything is imaginary.

C'est à cause de cette monotonie que la quantité joue un si grand rôle. Beaucoup de pouvoir, beaucoup de royaumes, beaucoup d'argent, beaucoup de femmes (don Juan) ou d'hommes (Célimène), etc. Condamné à la fausse infinité. C'est là l'enfer même. [82]

It is because of this monotony that *quantity* plays such a large role. Much power, many kingdoms, a lot of money, many women (Don Juan[37]) or men (Célimène[38]), etc. Condemned to an ersatz infinity. That is hell itself.

---

[37] Character created by Byron, 1788-1824, English Romantic poet.
[38] Character in the play *Le Misanthrope* by Molière (Jean Baptiste Poquelin), 1622-1673, French actor and dramatist.

Littérature et morale. Le mal imaginaire est romantique, romanesque, varié; le mal réel morne, monotone, désertique, ennuyeux. Le bien imaginaire est ennuyeux; le bien réel est toujours nouveau, merveilleux, enivrant. Donc la « littérature d'imagination » est ou ennuyeuse, ou immorale (ou un mélange des deux). Elle n'échappe à cette alternative qu'en passant en quelque sorte, à force de l'art, du coté de la réalité — ce que le génie seul peut faire. [83]

Literature and morality. Imaginary evil is romantic, fanciful, varied; real evil is dreary, monotonous, dry, boring. Imaginary good is boring; the truly good is always new, marvelous, intoxicating. Therefore the "literature of the imagination" is either boring or immoral (or a mixture of the two). It escapes this alternative only by passing over in some way, by the sheer force of art, to the side of reality — which genius alone can do.[39]

---

[39] "[F]olks expect of the poet [...] to indicate the path between reality and their souls." Walt Whitman, *Leaves of Grass*.

Ce que le mal viole, ce n'est pas le bien, car le bien est inviolable; on ne viole qu'un bien dégradé. [83]

What is violated by evil is not the good, for the good is inviolable; only a debased good can be violated.[40]

---

[40] "Absolute good is something other than the good that is the contrary and the correlative of evil, although it is its model and source." S.W., *Écrits de Londres et dernières lettres*, p. 102.

Le faux dieu change la souffrance en violence. Le vrai Dieu change la violence en souffrance. [86]

The false god changes suffering into violence. The true God changes violence into suffering.

Accepter le mal qu'on nous fait comme remède à celui que nous avons fait. [87]

Accept the evil that is done to us as the remedy for the evil we have done.

La joie est la plénitude du sentiment du réel. [96]

Joy is the full experience of what is real.

Quiconque prend l'épée périra par l'épée. Et quiconque ne prend pas l'épée (ou la lâche) périra sur la croix. [103]

Whoever takes up the sword will perish by the sword. And whoever does not take up the sword (or lays it down) will perish on the cross.[41]

---

[41] Matthew 26.52.

Nulle poésie concernant le peuple n'est authentique si la fatigue n'y est pas, et la faim et la soif issues de la fatigue. Leur dire: le Christ a été fatigué. [205]

No poetry about ordinary people[42] is authentic if weariness has no part in it, and the hunger and the thirst produced by weariness. Tell them: Christ was weary.

---

[42] "Just as people need bread, so do they need poetry [...] they need the daily substance of their lives to be poetry [...] This poetry can only be religion." S.W., in *La vie de Simone Weil*, p. 611.

Intuitions pré-Chrétiennes
Pre-Christian Intuitions

Simone Weil and God's Quest
in Sophocles and Aeschylus[43]

I. The Quest of Man by God
Hymn to Demeter[44]

I begin to sing of rich-haired Demeter, awful goddess -- of her and her trim-ankled daughter whom Aidoneus [Hades] rapt away, given to him by all-seeing Zeus the loud-thunderer. Apart from Demeter, lady of the golden sword and glorious fruits, she was playing with the deep-bosomed daughters of Oceanus and gathering flowers over a soft meadow, roses and crocuses and beautiful violets, irises also and hyacinths and the narcissus which Earth made to grow at the will of Zeus and to please the Host of Many, to be a snare for the bloom-like girl -- a marvellous, radiant flower. It was a thing of awe whether for deathless gods or mortal men to see: from its root grew a hundred blooms and it smelled most sweetly, so that all wide heaven above and the whole earth and the sea's salt swell laughed for joy. And the girl was amazed and reached out with both hands to take the lovely toy; but the wide-pathed earth yawned

---

[43] *Intuitions pré-Chrétiennes, pp. 9-13; 15-18; 20-21.*
[44] Translated by Hugh G. Evelyn-White (1914).

there in the plain of Nysa, and the lord, Host of Many, with his immortal horses sprang out upon her -- the Son of Cronos, He who has many names.

He caught her up reluctant on his golden car and bare her away lamenting. Then she cried out shrilly with her voice, calling upon her father, the Son of Cronos, who is most high and excellent. But no one, either of the deathless gods or of mortal men, heard her voice, nor yet the olive-trees bearing rich fruit: only tenderhearted Hecate, bright-coiffed, the daughter of Persaeus, heard the girl from her cave, and the lord Helios, Hyperion's bright son, as she cried to her father, the Son of Cronos. But he was sitting aloof, apart from the gods, in his temple where many pray, and receiving sweet offerings from mortal men. So he, that Son of Cronos, of many names, who is Ruler of Many and Host of Many, was bearing her away by leave of Zeus on his immortal chariot -- his own brother's child and all unwilling.

(*The sorrow of Demeter keeps the wheat from growing; humankind would perish and the gods would be without honor if Zeus does not send word to Hades to let the young girl leave. Hades, smiling, hears the message and obeys. He says to* Core[45]:)

"Go now, Persephone, to your dark-robed mother, go, and feel kindly in your heart towards me: be not so exceedingly cast down; for I shall be no unfitting husband for you among the deathless gods, that am own brother to father Zeus. And while you are here, you shall rule all that lives and moves and shall have the greatest rights among the deathless gods: those who defraud you and do not appease your power with offerings, reverently performing rites and paying fit gifts, shall be punished for evermore."

When he said this, wise Persephone was filled with joy and hastily sprang up for gladness. But he on his part secretly gave her sweet pomegranate seed to eat, taking care for himself that she might not remain continually with grave, dark-robed Demeter.

---

[45] Another name for Persephone.

(From then on she spends ⅔ of the year at the side of her mother, with the gods, ⅓ at the side of Hades.)

Simone Weil's Commentary[46]

Hades or Aidoneus, a name which means Invisible or Eternal, or both, appears sometimes as the brother of Zeus and sometimes as Zeus himself, for there is a subterranean Zeus. The name Demeter very probably means Mother Earth, and Demeter is identical with all those mother goddesses whose cult has so many analogies with the role played by the Virgin according to the Catholic conception. The narcissus is the flower that represents Narcissus, this being who is so beautiful that he can only love himself. The only beauty that could be an object of love for itself, that could be its own object, is the beauty of God. The soul seeking pleasure encounters the beauty of God which appears here below in the form of the beauty of the world as a trap for the soul. With the help of this trap, God seizes the soul despite itself. This is the same idea found in Plato's *Phaedrus*.[47] God must let the soul go back to nature, but before, by surprise, he secretly makes it eat a pomegranate

---

[46] This and the Commentaries by Weil which follow are translations by GAB.
[47] *Phaedrus* 250e.

seed. If it eats, it is possessed forever. The pomegranate seed is the consent the soul gives to God almost without its knowledge and without admitting it; it is like an infinitely tiny little thing among all the carnal inclinations of the soul, and yet it decides forever the soul's destiny. It is the mustard seed to which Christ compares the kingdom of heaven, the smallest of seeds but which later will become a tree where the birds of the air will nest.[48]

In this myth there are two successive acts of violence committed by God on the soul, the one is pure violence, the other for which the consent of the soul to God is indispensable and which decides its salvation. These two moments are found in the myth of *Phaedrus* and in that of the Cave.[49] They correspond to the parable in the Gospel concerning the Wedding Feast, for which guests are sought by chance along the highways, but for which only those with a wedding garment can remain, and they correspond to the opposition be-

---

[48] Matthew 13.31-32; Mark 4.31-32; Luke 13.19.
[49] *Republic* 7.514ff, 532ff.

tween "the called" and "the elect,"[50] and finally they correspond to the parable of the virgins who all go to find the groom but of whom only those who have oil are admitted.[51]

The idea of a trap set by God for man is also the meaning of the myth of the labyrinth,[52] if the stories added later about the wars between Crete and Athens are eliminated. Minos, the son of Zeus, judge of the dead, is this unique being whose names in antiquity are Osiris, Dionysus, Prometheus, Eros, Hermes, Apollo, and many others (the likelihood of these assimilations can be established). The Minotaur is the same being represented by the bull, just as Osiris is represented by the steer Apis and Dionysus-Zagreus[53] with horns (a symbolism connected with the moon and its phases can explain this image). The labyrinth is that path in which man, as soon as he enters it,

---

[50] Matthew 22.1-14; 20.16.

[51] Matthew 25.1-13.

[52] According to Greek mythology King Minos of Crete ordered a labyrinth to be built by Daedalus, an Athenian craftsman, architect, and inventor, in which the Minotaur, a man-eating creature, half-bull and half-man, was to be imprisoned.

[53] Another name for Dionysus.

loses his way and finds himself after a period of time unable either to retrace his steps or to go somewhere else. He wanders and roams without knowing where and finally comes to the place where God is waiting to eat him.

II. The Recognition of God and Man
Sophocles: Electra[54]

ELECTRA And where is that unhappy one's tomb?

ORESTES There is none; the living have no tomb.

ELECTRA What sayest thou, boy?

ORESTES Nothing that is not true.

ELECTRA The man is alive?

ORESTES If there be life in me.

ELECTRA What? Art thou he?

ORESTES Look at this signet, once our father's, and judge if I speak truth.

ELECTRA O blissful day!

---

[54] Translated by R. C. Jebb (1873).

ORESTES Blissful, in very deed!

ELECTRA Is this thy voice?

ORESTES Let no other voice reply.

ELECTRA Do I hold thee in my arms?

ORESTES As mayest thou hold me always!

ELECTRA Ah, dear friends and fellow-citizens, behold Orestes here, who was feigned dead, and now, by that feigning hath come safely home!

Simone Weil's Commentary

If these verses are read without thinking of the story of Electra and Orestes, the mystical resonance is obvious (hear it from no other voice — never again to part). If after that the story as it appears in Sophocles is thought of, the evidence becomes greater.

It is a matter of recognition, a frequent theme in folklore. One believes to have before oneself a stranger and it is the most beloved. This is what took place between Mary Magdalene and a certain gardener.[55]

Electra is the daughter of a powerful king, but reduced to the most miserable state of slavery on the orders of those who have betrayed her father. She is hungry. She is in rags. Affliction not only oppresses her but degrades and embitters her. But she does not give in. She hates these enemies of her father who have complete power over her. Only her brother who is far away could save her. She is consumed by the waiting. Finally he comes but

---

[55] Cf. John 20.15.

she is unaware of it. She believes she is seeing a stranger who announces his death and carries his ashes. She falls into a boundless despair, she wants to die. But even though she no longer hopes for anything, not for one instant does she dream of giving up. She only hates her enemies the more intensely. While she is holding the urn, weeping, Orestes, who had taken her for a slave, recognizes her by her tears. He tells her that the urn is empty. He reveals himself to her.

There is a double recognition. God recognizes the soul by her tears and then he allows himself to be recognized.

It is when the exhausted soul has ceased to expect God, when outer affliction or inner aridity makes her believe that God is not a reality; if, in spite of that, she continues to love him, if she has a horror of the good things here below that would replace him: it is then that God, after a while, comes to her, shows himself, speaks to her, touches her. This is what Saint John of the Cross calls the dark night.

Moreover, this grief poured out on the urn and the ashes of Orestes, followed by the joy of recognition, evokes as clearly as possible the theme of God dead and resurrected. One verse points to this theme without ambiguity:

mēchanaisi men thanonta,
nun de mēchanais sesōsmenon;

a stratagem has made him die,
at present a stratagem has saved him.

[Or, as above: *dead in craft,*
and now by craft restored to life again.]

But "stratagem" is not accurate. The word *mēchanē* is used by the tragedians, Plato, Pindar, Herodotus, in many texts which have a relationship, clear or hidden, direct or indirect, certain or conjectural, with the notions of salvation and redemption, notably in the *Prometheus*. The fact that this word was used in the mysteries makes this point plausible. This word means method and is a synonym for the word *poros* (concerning which see the commentary on the myth of the birth of Eros in the *Symposium*). This word is clearly used in a text of Herodotus in reference to the Passion. The corresponding Latin word is *machina*, and one applies the expression *Deus ex machina* to the god who comes down from above onto the stage at the end of a theatrical play

Sophocles is the poet in whom the Christian quality of inspiration is the most obvious and perhaps the most pure. (To the best of my knowledge, he is far more Christian than any other tragic poet of the last twenty centuries.)

III. The Operation of Grace
Aeschylus: Agamemnon[56]

The Chorus: Zeus, whosoever he be, — if by this name it well pleases him to be invoked, by this name I call to him — as I weigh all things in the balance, I can conjecture none save "Zeus," if in very truth I needs must cast aside this vain burden from my heart.

But whosoever, heartily taking thought beforehand, gives victory in triumphant shout to "Zeus," he shall gain wisdom altogether, — Zeus, who leads mortals the way of understanding, Zeus, who has established as a fixed ordinance that "wisdom comes by suffering." But even as trouble, bringing memory of pain, drops over the mind in sleep, so to men in their despite comes wisdom.[57] With constraint comes the grace of the powers divine enthroned upon their awesome seats.

---

[56] Translated H. Weir Smyth (1926).
[57] Or, *without their willing it wisdom came* (GAB).

Simone Weil's Commentary

"Zeus" no longer designates a particular divinity, just the word, "theos." Moreover they are from the same root. Besides, his name is unknown which [...] implies that it cannot be attained, unlike the false gods. We can only turn our thought toward him, and that suffices to obtain perfection.

"The memory of pain" means, according to the Orphic vocabulary, a premonition of eternal happiness, of the divine destiny of the soul. This premonition is distilled drop by drop in the sleep of unawareness; when one becomes aware, one is already possessed by grace and it only remains for the soul to consent. This image of the working of grace is consistent with the myth of Core (Persephone).

Bibliography

Works by Simone Weil in French

Attente de Dieu. Préface de J.M. Perrin. Paris: Librairie Arthème Fayard, 1966.

La Connaissance surnaturelle. Collection ESPOIR, dirigée par Albert Camus. Paris: Gallimard, 1950.

Écrits de Londres et dernières lettres. Paris: Éditions Gallimard, 1957.

L'Enracinement: Prélude à une déclaration des devoirs envers l'être humain. Paris: Éditions Gallimard, 1949.

Intuitions pré-chrétiennes. Paris: Librairie Arthème Fayard, 1985.

Leçons de philosophie. Presenté par Anne Reynaud-Guérithault. Préface de Jean Guitton. Paris: Plon, 1989.

Lettre à un religieux. Introduction par Jean-Pie Lapierre. Paris: Éditions Gallimard, 1951.

Œuvres complètes. Publié sous la direction d'André Devaux et Florence de Lussy. Paris: Éditions Gallimard, 1988--.

Tome I. Premiers écrits philosophiques, 1988.

Tome II. Écrits historiques et politiques.

Volume 1. L'Engagement syndical, 1988.

Volume 2. L'Expérience ouvrière et l'adieu à la révolution, 1991.

Volume 3. Vers la guerre, 1989.

Tome IV. Écrits de Marseille.

Volume 1. 1940-1942, 2008.

Volume 2. 1941-1942, 2009.

Tome V. Écrits de New York et de Londres

Volume 2. 1943, 2013

Tome VI. Cahiers

Volume 1. Cahiers I-III (1933-9/1941), 1994.

Volume 2. Cahiers IV-VII (9/1941-2/1942), 1997.

Volume 3. Cahiers VIII-XII (2/1942-6/1942), 2002.

Volume 4. Cahiers XIII-XVIII (7/1942-7/1943), 2006.

Tome VII. Correspondence

Volume 1. Correspondence Familiale, 2012.

La pesanteur et la grâce. Préface de Gustave Thibon. Paris: Plon, 1988.

Réflexions sur les causes de la liberté et de l'oppression sociale. Paris: Éditions Gallimard, 1955.

Works by Simone Weil in translation

Awaiting God. A New Translation of *Attente de Dieu* and *Lettre à un Religieux* by Bradley Jersak, with an Introduction by Sylvie Weil. Abbotsford, BC: Fresh Wind Press, 2012.

Escritos de Londres y últimas cartas. Traducción de Maite Larrauri. Madrid: Editorial Trotta, 2000.

First and Last Notebooks. Translated by Richard Rees. London: Oxford University Press, 1970.

Formative Writings. Edited and translated by Dorothy Tuck McFarland and Wilhelmina Van Ness. London: Routledge & Kegan Paul, 1987.

Gateway to God. Edited by David Raper, with the collaboration of Malcolm Muggeridge and Vernon Sproxton. New York: Crossroad, 1982.

Gravity and Grace. Translated by Arthur Wills, with Introductions by Gustave Thibon and Thomas R. Nevin. Lincoln: University of Nebraska Press, 1997.

"The *Iliad* or the Poem of Force." In *Revisions: Changing Perspectives in Moral Philosophy.* Edited by Stanley Hauerwas and Alasdair MacIntyre. Notre Dame, IN: University of Notre Dame Press, 1983, pp. 222-248.

Intimations of Christianity Among the Ancient Greeks. London: Ark Paperbacks, 1987.

Lectures on Philosophy. Translated by Hugh Price, with an Introduction by Peter Finch. Cambridge:

Cambridge University Press, 1993.

Letter to a Priest. Penguin Books, 2003.

The Need for Roots. Translated by Arthur Wills, with a Preface by T.S. Eliot. London: Routledge, 1995.

The Notebooks. Volume One. Translated by Arthur Wills. New York: G.P. Putnam's Sons, 1956.

The Notebooks. Volume Two. Translated by Arthur Wills. New York: G.P. Putnam's Sons, 1956.

Oppression and Liberty. Translated by Arthur Wills and John Petrie, with an Introduction by F.C. Ellert. Amherst, MA: The University of Massachusetts Press, 1973.

Pensamientos desordenados. Traducción de María Tabuyo y Augustín López. Madrid: Trotta, 1995.

Selected Essays. Chosen and Translated by Richard Rees. London: Oxford University Press, 1962.

Seventy Letters. Translated and arranged by Richard Rees. London: Oxford University Press, 1965.

Simone Weil: An Anthology. Edited and introduced by Siân Miles. New York: Weidenfeld & Nicholson, 1986.

The Simone Weil Reader. Edited by George A. Panichas. Mt. Kisco, NY: Moyer Bell Limited, 1977.

Simone Weil. Writings selected with an Introduction by Eric O. Springsted. Maryknoll, NY: Orbis Books, 1998.

Waiting For God. Translated by Emma Craufurd, with an Introduction by Leslie Fiedler. New York: Harper & Row, 1973.

War and the Iliad. Simone Weil and Rachel Bespaloff. Translated by Mary McCarthy, with an Introduction by Christopher Benfey and an Essay by Hermann Broch. New York: New York Review Books, 2005.

Works about Simone Weil

Abosch, Heinz. *Simone Weil: An Introduction.* Translated from the German by Kimberly A. Kinny. New York: Pennbridge Books, 1994.

Allen, Diogenes. *Three Outsiders: Søren Kierkegaard, Blaise Pascal, Simone Weil.* Cambridge, MA: Cowley Publications, 1983.

Allen, Diogenes and Eric O. Springsted. *Spirit, Nature, and Community: Issues in the Thought of Simone Weil.* Albany, NY: State University of New York Press, 1994.

Bell, Richard H. *Simone Weil: The Way of Justice as Compassion.* Lanham, MD: Rowman & Littlefield, 1998.

Blum, Lawrence A. and Victor J. Seidler. *A Truer Liberty. Simone Weil and Marxism.* London: Routledge, 1989.

Brenner, Rachel Feldhay. *Writing as Resistence. Four Women Confronting the Holocaust.* University Park, PA: PA State University Press, 1997.

Brueck, Katherine T. "The Mysticism of Simone Weil and François Mauriac's Viper's Tangle: Affliction, Gravity, and Grace." *Mystics Quarterly.* Volume XV, Number 4, December 1989, pp. 166-175.

Brueck, Katherine T. *The Redemption of Tragedy: The Literary Vision of Simone Weil.* Albany, NY: State University of New York Press, 1995.

Buber, Martin. "The Silent Question." In *At The Turning.* New York: Farrar, Straus and Young, 1952, pp. 27-44.

Cabaud, Jacques. *L'Expérience vécue de Simone Weil.* Paris: Plon, 1957.

Cabaud, Jacques. *A Fellowship of Love.* New York: Channel Press, 1964.

Chenavier, Robert. *Simone Weil. Attention to the Real.* Translated by Bernard E. Doering. Notre Dame, IN: University of Notre Dame Press, 2012.

Cliff, Michelle. "Sister/Outsider: Some Thoughts on Simone Weil." In *Between Women.* Edited by

Carol Ascher, Louise DeSalvo, Sara Ruddick. New York: Routlege, 1993, pp. 311-325.

Coles, Robert. *Simone Weil: A Modern Pilgrimage.* Reading, MA: Addison-Wesley Publishing Co, 1989.

Daniels, Kate. "The Testimony of Simone Weil." *Four Testimonies: Poems.* Baton Rouge, LA: Louisiana State University Press, 1998, pp. 1-25.

Dargan, Joan. *Simone Weil: Thinking Poetically.* Albany, NY: State University of New York Press, 1999.

Davy, Marie-Magdeleine. *The Mysticism of Simone Weil.* Translated by Cynthia Rowland. Boston: The Beacon Press, 1951.

Dietz, Mary G. *Between the Human and the Divine: The Political Thought of Simone Weil.* Totowa, NJ: Rowman and Littlefield, 1988.

Dinnage, Rosemary. "Feeding on Light: Simone Weil." *Alone! Alone. Lives of Some Outsider Women.* New York: New York Review Books, 2004, pp. 37-50.

Dunaway, John M. and Eric O. Springsted, Editors. *The Beauty That Saves: Essays on Aesthetics and Language in Simone Weil.* Macon, GA: Mercer University Press, 1996.

Finch, Henry Leroy. *Simone Weil and the Intellect of Grace*. Edited by Martin Andic. New York: Continuum, 1999.

Fiori, Gabriella. *Simone Weil: An Intellectual Biography*. Translated by Joseph R. Berrigan. Athens, GA: The University of Georgia Press, 1989.

Greene, Graham. "Simone Weil." In *Collected Essays*. London: Penguin, 1969, 1988, pp. 279-282.

Grote, Jim. "Weil's Theory of Social Force." In *Spirituality Today*. Vol. 42, No. 3, Autumn 1990, pp. 217-232.

Hellman, John. *Simone Weil: An Introduction to Her Thought*. Waterloo, ON: Wilfrid Laurier University Press, 1982.

Hohlwein, Kathryn. "Armed with a Burning Patience: Reflections on Simone Weil." In *The Feminist Mystic and Other Essays on Women and Spirituality*. Edited by Mary E. Giles. New York: Crossroad, 1985, pp. 142-157.

Irwin, Alexander. *Saints of the Impossible: Bataille, Weil, and the Politics of the Sacred*. Minneapolis: Minnesota University Press, 2002.

Klassen, Sarah. *Simone Weil: Songs of Hunger and Love*. Toronto: Wolsak and Wynn, 1999.

McLellan, David. *Utopian Pessimist: The Life and*

Thought of Simone Weil. New York: Poseidon Press, 1990.

Milosz, Czeslaw. "The Importance of Simone Weil." In *To Begin Where I Am. Selected Essays*. Edited and with an Introduction by Bogdana Carpenter and Madeline G. Levine. New York: Farrar, Straus and Giroux, 2001, pp. 246-259.

Miollis, Jean de. *La passion de la verité*. Paris: Téqui, 1999.

Molinaro, Ursule. "Simone Weil." *A Full Moon of Women*. New York: Dutton, 1990, pp. 87-91.

Morgan, Vance G. *Weaving The World. Simone Weil on Science, Mathematics, and Love*. Notre Dame, IN: University of Notre Dame Press, 2005.

Moulakis, Athanasios. *Simone Weil and the Politics of Self-Denial*. Translated from the German by Ruth Hein. Columbia, MO: University of Missouri Press, 1998.

Nava, Alexander. *The Mystical and Prophetic Thought of Simone Weil and Gustavo Gutiérrez*. Albany, NY: State University of New York Press, 2001.

Nevin, Thomas. *Simone Weil: Portrait of a Self-Exiled Jew*. Chapel Hill, NC: The University of North Carolina Press, 1991.

Nordquist, Joan. *Simone Weil: A Bibliography.* Santa Cruz, CA: Reference and Research Services, 1995.

Nye, Andrea. *Philosophia: The Thought of Rosa Luxemburg, Simone Weil, and Hannah Arendt.* London: Routledge, 1994.

Oxenhandler, Neal. *Looking for Heroes in Postwar France: Albert Camus, Max Jacob, Simone Weil.* Hanover, NH: Dartmouth College, 1996.

Patsouras, Louis. *Simone Weil and the Socialist Tradition.* San Francisco: EMText, 1992.

Perrin, J.M. and G. Thibon. *Simone Weil telle que nous l'avons connue.* Paris: Éditions du Vieux Colombier, 1952.

Perrin, J.M. and G. Thibon. *Simone Weil as We Knew Her.* Paris: Translated by Emma Craufurd. London: Routledge, 1953, reprint 2003.

Pétrement, Simone. *La vie de Simone Weil.* Paris: Librairie Arthème Fayard, 1973.

Pétrement, Simone. *Simone Weil: A Life.* Translated by Raymond Rosenthal. New York: Pantheon Books, 1976.

Plant, Stephen. *Simone Weil.* Liguori, MO: Triumph, 1996.

Question de Simone Weil: Le Grand Passage. Ed.

Marc de Smedt. Paris: Albin Michel, 1994.

Rees, Richard. *Simone Weil: A Sketch for a Portrait.* Carbondale, IL: Southern Illinois University Press, 1978.

Réponses aux Questions de Simone Weil. Paris, Aubier, 1964.

Rhees, Rush. *Discussions of Simone Weil.* Edited by D.Z. Phillips and Mario von der Ruhr. Albany, NY: State University of New York Press, 2000.

Rozelle-Stone, A. Rebecca and Lucian Stone, eds. *The Relevance of the Radical. Simone Weil 100 Years Later.* London & New York: Continuum, 2010.

Rozelle-Stone, A. Rebecca and Lucian Stone. S*imone Weil and Theology.* London: Bloomsbury, 2013.

Sontag, Susan. "Simone Weil." In *Against Interpretation.* New York: Doubleday, 1990, pp. 49-51.

Springsted, Eric O. *Christus Mediator: Platonic Mediation in the Thought of Simone Weil.* Chico, CA: Scholars Press, 1983.

Springsted, Eric O. *Simone Weil and the Suffering of Love,* with a Preface by Robert Coles. Cambridge, MA: Cowley Publications, 1986.

Stokes, Thomas. *Audience, Attention and Rhetoric*

in Pascal and Simone Weil. New York: Peter Lang, 1996.

Strickland, Stephanie. *The Red Virgin: A Poem of Simone Weil*. Madison, WI: The University of Wisconsin Press, 1993.

Terry, Megan. *Approaching Simone*. Old Westbury, NY: The Feminist Press, 1973.

Vetö, Miklos. *The Religious Metaphysics of Simone Weil*. Translated by Joan Dargan. Albany, NY: State University of New York Press, 1994.

Weil, Sylvie. *At Home with André and Simone Weil*. Translated by Benjamin Ivry. Evanston: Northwestern University Press, 2010.

White, George Abbott, Editor. *Simone Weil: Interpretations of a Life*. Amherst, MA: The University of Massachusetts Press, 1981.

Winch, Peter. *Simone Weil. "The Just Balance."* Cambridge: Cambridge University Press, 1989.

Yourgrau, Palle. *Simone Weil*. London: Reaktion Books, 2011.

Film and Music

Haslett, Julia. *An Encounter with Simone Weil* , 2010.

Katz, Darrell and Paul Taturinis. *The Death of*

Simone Weil. Nova, 2002.

Other Works by the Translator
Available at Amazon in the U.S. and abroad

Lines of Inquiry (Verse), alphabetical listing:
- *Blue Book 2003-2005*
- *Blue Book 2006*
- *Blue Book 2007*
- *Blue Book 2008*
- *Claiborne Creek*
- *Crossings*
- *Fractions*
- *Lily*
- *Preservations*
- *Reflections*
- *Resolutions*
- *Roselawn Place*
- *Seasons of Blue*
- *South on LA 1*
- *Zoe I*
- *Zoe II*
- *Zoe III*

In preparation:
- *Blue Book 2009*
- *Blue Book 2010*

- *Blue Book 2011*
- *Blue Book 2012*
- *Blue Book 2013*

Translations (*en face*)

- *Cries of the Heart and Other Excited Utterances*

Selected passages from
[1] the Septuagint and New Testament
   (Greek-English)
[2] Dionysios the Areopagite
       (Greek-English)
[3] Richard Rolle
       (Latin-English)
[4] The author of *The Cloud of Unknowing*
       (Middle English-Modern English)
[5] John of the Cross
       (Spanish-English)
[6] Jean-Pierre de Caussade
       (French-English)

- *Simone Weil: Wrestling with God*
  French-English texts (*en face*)
  Selected from the works of Simone Weil

- *Simone Weil: Bilingual Essays*
  French-English texts (*en face*)
  [1] *Profession de Foi*
      Profession of Faith
  [2] *Autobiographie spirituelle*
      Spiritual Autobiography
  [3] *Réflexions sur le bon usage des études scolaires en vue de l'amour de Dieu*
      Reflections on the Good Use of School Studies as a Way to Come to a Love for God
  [4] *Cette Guerre est une guerre de religion*
      This War is a Religious War
  [5] *Réflexions sans ordre sur l'amour de Dieu*
      Various Reflections on the Love of God

- *The Mystical Theology of Dionysios the Areopagite. A Translator's Handbook*

Contents:

- Two Early 20th Century Translations
- Greek Language Aids
- Analytical Lexicon
- Paradigms
- The Greek Text
- Bibliography
- Appendix

L • JJ • B • W
HartWorks 2017
Zwn 10 Weil.doc

Printed in Great
Britain
by Amazon